LOVELY

LOVELY

CHU JIN

atmosphere press

To my beloved family

Table of Contents

Curiosity in Awe

what if i ask
no longer?

what if i think again? what if i
wonder, like i did, about life and wisdom?

will i be forgotten as a little being
or gossiped as a little not-to-be

yet lively?

Picnic on Tuesday

you were to me a park,

leisure,
airs around,
chaos behind.

i walked in, as you chose me,
to wear the scent
of the spring belated.

Love is a sweet anarchy

love is an explosion

of associations.
love eludes

understanding.
love must inflame

a tendency;
it extinguishes it,
sings for it.

Attentions

i'd love you

sensibly,
as if a blooming valley,
as if bells celebrating,

as if the nature of love,

as if a summer,
but warmly,
but tenderly,

consistently,
without making your heart split
open,

without a vagueness.

Lovers' whispers, aphoristic

love is no more than a mysterious

hierarchy
of symbolism, luscious.

we are enemies to hide;
to reveal,
we're the masters

of that of the other.

—then how
did we ever come to speak it
as though it's apprehensible?

Garden of Eden

during the day,
i followed the light sprinkled
over your shoulders. the hilltop
was the only crown in the universe,
i was the last sweet joy here; you all the rosy.
during the night,
i followed the glinting flow
that was ascending; with a fragrance
it descended between the hot,
if not too chill,

between us.

after years,
i realized it was the moon
forgetting herself; the moon shadowed
the surface of the blue pearl lake
of your eyes sinking
into the floor at the bottom of my heart;
the fairyland was seldom revisited.

What else should lovers wonder not?

stealth. boredom barely survives
secrecy. this is the thing plainly boring.

Wrong prophet

i talked to the mediocre
i met. i don't listen to it.

i'd rather play

with the odds
of shame and waves of laughs.

Happy together

we had a thing
bizarre;

too bizarre to be announced
as love as they defined it.

we didn't know it.
we loved beyond

what love should be named.

Don't break my heart

i was a disciple. in your masked absences,
i prized you the award should not be a thing

desired and unwanted.

Hypocrisy

we were loyal as if one duo
separated long yet unified
until our silent souls were occupied
fully,
by a silently touching translucency.

In the cave

on some days, you made me free of scare;
on the rest of the days, i waited and waited.

It goes on

you have a gracious
origin. a divine game.

all the rest suspends. a good rest.

A written manifestation

i liked the breezes on the day
you led me there,
to the facade of the sea.
without a wave. tremendous.

i liked the time praying,
when we stayed
a bit longer under the milky way.
we sketched the gestures of stars.

i liked the first song you played
when you caught me. disfigured the fear
you made arise in my faith. there,
i liked the rhyme as if it would resound
every moment when i failed to hide
my sincerest praying to it.

Endgame

the old pictures are still exactly bright,
but we let them keep their words unheard.

we won't laugh again
at the same joke;

we'd dealt with it.

The Island and its forest

at the end of the day,
i continued to write in a new light.

each footnote is a resonance
of the ears of poetry you knitted
my heart with. as if the first
harvest, as if the first full moon,
as if each is a dawn in itself.

Second naivety

a noble lie in the world
satiates my yearning

eager for a sacred truth
that that's beautiful and good.

The remains of love

tell me
you're mad at me.

let my hearts get drippy
~ you know they'd not
belonged to my stifling wishes,

(you know you wanted me
to destroy this into submission)

when they're saturated
thoroughly
with firing airs

for reasons no less sweet.

Waves of springs

the gardens are exceptional;
unusual;

they come and go.
they ARE, but they cannot be,
as if an escape
from the form of purposes,
a deluge of untrue totalities.

Moments of doubts

i asked God
where
my winds will be.

i heard
the rustling sound of trees
faraway,

knowing nowhere, satisfied.

Apologies

the wisest sage teaches us,
"reason is to rule at the above."
then i've spent all my things
struggling against the other two.

i often failed to play with them
all. my lovings were monstrous.
i could barely think, or breathe then.

i thought he showed me the method
until i felt; he showed me his scab.

In tensions

they never allow
a single bad word;

they know precisely
the bad words.

Be fine

it's okay
if people state it's okay.

it's okay
if you point out
a few differences.

Flow in the soil

sometimes, i don't know
the whats and whys;
i know this.

i seem to adore
a wild perception so strange.
i seem to blame
an adoration out of

nothing i've known indeed.

Temple

every-time.
after all the humane,
nonsensical
sensualities,

i rest and settle
in a written remorse

that forgives
all uncertainties.

Stories of hearts

some hearts are
hearts.
they couldn't
theorize

why things fade;
why it only upsets them?

some look back
as if a sighing
without a speck of dust.

Natural

to get frightened when the ends befall.

they won't have been of more generosity
if I'd begged earlier and more wretchedly.

By the air of life

all my wildness is a parody

of a soul of heaven
whose being drifts onward,
as if a river, as if a montage,
as if a constancy, as if a new language.

A thinking

i'm a step away
from void,

but i have two paths.
void.
as if a void.

Love letter

things come from you,
things run towards you.
this is the only thing

we've agreed upon
as if you'd denied
my consents and denials.

Hopeful

stars fall.
we look upward
in grief. on this tedious night

as usual,
a beautiful soul is a ranger.

In the dim lights

when the light wanes,
the strings begin to sing

for each soul-
being.

some rise out of ashes.
some pray
there will be a peace
of a deep sea violet.

Questions and answers

at first, i was to seek
the gleaming golden stars.
later i saw them
slug-gish.
repulsive as this human body.

meanwhile, i could never know
to which side my soul is to greet.

Light

we want a richness.
we need it

to nourish our hearts
for a truer completeness.

Sweetness and lightness

we are sweetness and lightness
as if we are a heart and a soul.

Elf. my elf.

my little cloud. my
softest
wish. sweet,
look. i'm your third guardian
below a wise King. looking at me,
are you? i am
done with all the inquiries.

a pair of untouched eyes are so, so lovely.

About the Author

CHU JIN has a Ph.D. specializing in philosophy and aesthetics, and is currently pursuing a law degree. They reside in New York City.

In their leisure time, they enjoy indulging in Hong Kong street food, finding solace in the beloved character Paddington, and playing Final Fantasy XIV.